CSU Poetry Series LI

**Cleveland State University
Poetry Center**

Cocktails with Brueghel at the Museum Cafe

by **Sandra Stone**

Manufactured in the United States of America

Published by Cleveland State University Poetry Center
1983 E. 24th St., Cleveland, OH 44115-2440

ISBN 1-880834-26-X (cloth)
1-880834-25-1 (paper)

Library of Congress Catalog Card Number: 96-84737

Second Printing

For Lisa, Julie, and Adam

I The Mouth and Other Forms of Gravity

II Cocktails with Brueghel at the Museum Cafe

III My Artifacts, My Children, My Parents, My Books

IV The Woman with a List

V Ruminations on Concave Water

1

The Mouth and Other Forms of Gravity

March Already, I Must Give a Party

There's a reason for the house to resonate like this,
like a catacomb. Company's due.

I don't need an excuse to doll myself in clothes of the deceased,
to implant a vase with green lilies.

Mirthlessly now, the chime, the assembly, totemic on the doorstep,
the porch light's blaze, an inverted horn.

Shall we begin with the salver heaped with place cards,
our names impaled on a pin? A refuge, the niceties.

Please be so kind, would you be so kind
as to sink completely into the plumped sofas,

the scintillants over there. Tell me about your children
and lives, the one, so demonstrable.

I love the sycophantic murmur at the table,
the tyrannical eye of the connoisseur

fresh from the auction, don't you?
— the baffle of curators, conservators, aestheticians,

the *éminence grise,* that tenant with his salient wit,
the complement of picks and tongs,

bon mot and bon bons, salts in their cellars,
the ceaseless ping of crystal, don't you?

The banality of candles. Also, the flame that gutters,
globules that wax the limbs of inherited candlesticks,

that clog shallow pocks bored by artisans
to create an impression of worms,

where real mites are interred.
They nibble inaudibly, they impinge on my nerves.

A rote welcome to all.
A merciless *Chin Chin.*

The Resonance of Objects Litany

The three windows of my chamber
Ardor, Water, Sleep

Red Battery, Drunk Doubler, Poem of Three Worlds
The Casement, The Violent Reader

O Woman with Loud Treasures
Cold Vitrine, Gobbler, Sibilant Coverlet

Bound Rib, Cloche of Habit, Moth with Vague Smile
Amber snapshot, O Woman, You Object

Silk Topknot, my hair does not know me
Hair is not sentient

Woman, plus Clarity
I do not know how to plait my hair

The Three Windows of my Chamber
Ardor, Water, Sleep

Porch of September
The Receding Telescope

The curlicue my hair is
The object of my lens

Magnification, Hunger, that Troubadour
Ardor, Water, Sleep

The Mouth and Other Forms of Gravity

1

So much is known of the physical lives of rivers
that it does not need to be said how they lodge with us,
not just their names, their lighted mouths,
but their voices, the vocabulary they possess.
And what we know of *river,* we know like our mother tongue,
the peculiarities of its breath,
the rush of syllables when it's eased,
exact to our body, its contours, its odors, its lolligag.
We know how to stroke it, ways its course can be altered
with lingo we come hard by,
can cause it to submit, or revise itself
by trolling a hand in its flat eddies.

Isn't river hunger a human kind of enterprise
for leaping and subsiding?

2

Into the murk we peer with a kind of rapture. Isn't rapture
to press our ear to the layer of its skin, *river,*
to hear its garbled voice,
its erotic murmur beneath the surface
—a wish for shadowy depths?
            How it arches, yields, *river,*
when we crease it with dummy oars,
or snag its roots,
or stride it in our rustic gear,
our familiar waders,
or ply it with our craft, or personal decoys
that oblige it to warble.

3

We chart the course as we, only, perceive the course to be,
use navigator's toys to read the rapids, to be seduced
by given water that seems to smoke, given mornings,
vapors that seem to wrap it,
given dusks.

4

Rivers: their uses, their magnetic instruments
that register the frequency of light;
spot a some-time sun,
that lamp's grave gaze that bobs on glitter,
on debris of summer,
on those we love, disembarking,
their receding forms disheveling
on the river's mirrored back,
a futile lectern.

5

Certain photographers (that was a platinum process
that produced the sense of static time
we thumbed the album to see again
—the imagined box, its eye snapped shut,
stayed rapt entire years
and never really in our minds closed down)
love of darkrooms powered them,
on watch at rivers for vivid pockets
where life recurrently drapes its breath.

Our choice, to let current tow us,
river to course our veins from dock to dock,
an orphan destination,
to lift our mouths to other mouths, those magnets,
a form of gravity that draws us to it,
down to percussive water.

The Art of Crackage

By the way, those flowers, button size,
we bought at the stall?

Days later, blued numb, standing up to their knees
in pots too small for their imagined feet
couldn't even collapse
the way most living things decently do, finally,
but faded to a kind of dusk
that outlasted all but evening
in our evening mind.

The stone basin,
dependent for its mirror on rain, yesterday in the courtyard
unfilled itself. I suppose this is what is meant
by seepage, the barely perceived hairline crack,
the weathered days, one after one,
the sieve through which fathers baldly pass,
mother, with her badly conceived apron,
and, finally, ourselves, from wherever we were,
last seen by ourselves.

Will you say how you came to plant nothing
that ever seemed to persist
except maybe the idea of father,
that imposter in a business suit,
a second face we love, along with mother,
vanishing into the day's colander,
infinitely regressing,
apparitions in the courtyard at day's end,
their grave gaze in blue light?

        I prefer the face
behind its indifferent mask. And the body,
a sad scaffold. Or the heart, perched on a lifeguard's scan.
Because the flower folds sooner.
And father. And mother.

        Still, don't we go on
craving the sight of the face of the other?
Isn't this too bad, such hunger in the courtyard
for the reflection of what is lapsed or eluded,
vainly, for the sight of itself,
a small blue flower of no particularity, bent to an absence,
an unbearable crack, a report of the dark?

The Small a Table Is, Two Chairs Pulled Up

Gray in the courtyard. Windless.
No leaves float in the basin.
The stone is too porous for rain to pool.
What once was a mirror by which I knew myself
Lacks a face. Porosity is the cause.
And loss of illusion.

Not any season for falling out. No death
Between seasons I can mark. Ordinary days
Do not keen. Days have no funerals.
Days are without provenance. The calendar?
It's one after one, symmetric boxes,
Every one a small, a gray abyss.

I prefer the cutlass to the scythe.
To hack at the shoots, the skin of the earth,
Its sinews, gravel scattered in its jaws. What hunger
With its everywhere. Go on, I say to the leaf
That drifts to the chair.
Could you loft of your own volition?

Here in the courtyard where the dwarf bamboo
Sets up a clamor of green,
No contentious visitor knuckles the pane.
Where the moon unscrolls in Mr. Evening's room,
And pointlessly stakes the table for one,
No cobble groans, no gray small rain rains.

In the Night Parlor, Chair, Rain, Enigmatic Window

1

Sit with me. It is night again. That is the rain
that intermittently remarks, as you used to on that toy,
a prostrate without verse, without flower,
existences that live to celebrate, then die.

Who sanctions the rain? Who says it is all right for rain
to confer significance, little tympani,
too unremarkable to be irremediably sad,
a sad course down the trivial face night has become,
because Night is, after all,
the obverse body and its band.

The pane waters itself from some efficiency that has a name.
But what do I care for reason, for the nominative sciences?

Chair, define yourself. A ledger and four pins?
A disappointed throne?
Because the absented is an occupier,
and is remarkable for the shrill of its tenor,
no less than an imagined photograph in a real frame on the mantel,
the gaze from the frame, I mean, a devout,
like a bald eye,
              no less, all fidelities that survive the narrative,
its canny maneuvers,
the bankruptcy we tell ourselves the heart is,
Night, its revenant chaperone.

There is the altar of the inkpot, its paraphernalia,
the guest book with its embarrassing trills,
and rain, invisible music,
its rapid decrescendo
like the pulse,

or the calendar's inquiry,
its vivas,
the wall on which they are scratched.

2

That is the vacated chair, the book
whose protagonist keeps vigil,
the overseer lamp, its remorseless gaze.

Praise the irrelevant Mr. X,
the disembodied hand that absently strokes the penknife,
nerveless, benign.

Who inhabits the Chinese chair,
an ordinary presence, like dusk,
that derby-hatted caller?

Today is endurable on account of the rain,
and despite the rain,
an intermittent barterer.

But it is also a battering angel
of small rapture
because it is one motion in its short descent.

Game

It is a night like February, withholding light,
brittle with silences and snow, wind breaking against the baffles.

Your mind, my move.

Our hands splay at Ouija over empty answers.
Apple wine that checks our veins is dust in company of apples.

Is this harmless knowledge?
Benignly we touch, raise dust of apples.

My hand, your thrust.

We pulsate backwards from Z through July,
erasing lies and summer, equidistant from tonight,
the sorceries of sun and simple sex.
The Man with the Flower in His Mouth is smiling *cheese*,
is dancing on the lake, is shaking hands with daisies,
is falling off the platforms of the waves,
the tiny docks.

We waft. Wine flows like apples. Sun
the color of egg yolk spills across the grass.
Beyond the bounty of February rifts,
now bound for A, we rattle dust, swerve alphabets.
Unintentionally we are kind. The snow starts to lengthen.
A tacit agreement to begin bleak March
is meanwhile being formed.

Your word. My stand.

The Ballroom of Antiquity in Dreams

Who inhabits the dome, exquisite in her revolutions,
impaled on a pin animated by dust, staccato breath,
and recurrent tunes on the harmonium of the mind?

Nothing is new, finally, but recurs without motive, like a messenger,
and is borne out in a swoon.

Everything has happened, the tiny symbols in motion,
their formal guilt, their runes, the world over. Or, they appear
in armor, in the rusty patina of the beetle,
a stand-in for antiquity, in the shadow box, or bell jar,
or under duress in the splintered floorboards
of the blue-hour ballroom amid the customary sweepings.

In the aerie, French doors give onto lawn
like a carved jape. There is the rustic gazebo,
violet in afterdusk, the lavender wisteria
on a ladder in front of the moon.
All this has been waltzed to times before,
in the mirrored gaze the eye is,
that flattering ballroom with blinkers.

Then, too, the whisperings. That would be from the corridor,
its paneling applied, as the sheath is to a Chinese box,
its concealed drawers,
the secret letter reposited,
the mites that teem in its folds,
their virtually silent consumption,

or, from the mannered figurine of ivory,
civilized by a master artisan
whose fingers re-enact the dance. Nothing happens
that has not happened,
as historians know with anterior eyes.

Now it remains the task to awaken to the beatitude
that precedes real waking, and to be awake,
and to dispatch the messenger,
that elliptic, receding,
with whose visage and bearing you remain obsessed,
with whose . . .

Breathe, breathe. Suffocate the messenger.

Punctuation

Is that you also who have come to this place
looking for the right form?

Don't hold your hat in your hand
like that. Speak up!

Perhaps it is a letter of explanation
you want to leave,

a calling card?
An object of ambiguous meaning?

Perhaps it is a voice you want to call up,
or a loved tattoo.

Perhaps, to explore the tactics of bereavement
you want an inventive grammar.

For the obsequies, an impromptu.
May I be of some help?

See that you oblige your body, like a comma,
over what was used to be called

a mound. For innuendo, let me
commend to you the ellipsis,

a form of exquisite
absence ....

And the semicolon; its continuance
is like a mouth,

sinuous, interdependent.
But the comma,

inverted,
is like a mound.

The hyphen—it links
the amorously wracked

in a fractional embrace.
The exclamation point precedes

surrender! But the comma,
is banal.

Body, that old saw, in its nightly clamor,
its hue and outcry,

its exquisite handwringing
is like the poet.

Nothing is more improper
than to make of yourself

a tiny drama, punctuated
improperly,

drawing your breath from
the moss on the slab.

Period.

Governance

These random condolences.

A complicitous glance, a hand,
a wilted flower in a sack marked paid.
Of what use are they?

And the governing body?
Its simple wants are explicit:
Someone to lie with, strategic arms, wild mouth.

It rained last night. I went out to see what was tainted.
I warned myself not to drink from a leaf. And not to be thirsty.
And not to eat anything that feeds on grass. And not to want feeding.

I ordered my body terse. And self-consoled.
Intransigent weather, a siege lieutenant,
a wily solicitor.

What have I taught myself to forget?

Amatory Salute

I want to be negligent tonight in front of the eye of the fire,
that bounder with a single eye, falsely hot.

Let me be negligent as a flare for myself, that searer,
negligently to cast my shadow, a wanton,

in front of that singed eye,
lascivious in its glow.

I am stunned by its fiery narrative,
its salutary tongue.

II

Cocktails with Brueghel at the Museum Cafe

Cocktails with Brueghel at the Museum Cafe

1

To slip through the turnstile? To tuck in my blouson?
To become so ... indistinguishable?

Look here, what a motley—but then, weren't we all
always also seeking refreshment? No novelty—
groats, served on a door.

Let them stare. I don't mind being diminutive,
being one of the little throng humbled by the body's trek. Should I?

So what, me with my gnarled root, knobbed to my palm.
Better yet, my notched stick hacked from the living tree
than a shopping bag jammy.
Anyway, a sapless limb tucked to my thigh.
It could be every age has a prop—a delusion, eh? a hump,
a scurvy appendage,
a cackle, a rheumy eye.

It must be they've gussied up the gallery. For a carnival,
am I right?
            The body, frocked, in its pitiless course,
doesn't seem to have changed all that much. So much then
for the pity of art. But what *do* these blunderers from the village do,
perched uneasy? Winter here at the cafe? I grant you,
a three-legged stool is more stout than a swivel,
a mug, than a spindly stem. But, so? Every age wants bucking.

Who's that in the mirror? Oh, that will be me,
although I was not quite able to make me out in the crush,
dwarfed as I am. My sleeves, bunched at the wrist,
obscure the ankle of the glass history can't quaff from
because it will snap.

And here we are, and here we are, everywhere jostled,
elbow to elbow, our thirst unslaked,
some event like a carbuncle affixed to our affairs.

You call this a *goblet?* Let's raise ours, then, for you know, master,
what we see in the glass is what goes on.

I hobble about in the patch of red shift you gave me, master,
a flick, a flicker, really, of immaterial crimson
in the madcap course,
a dwarfed person with a chit from the curator,
animated by a decent red, with a—what's this you call it—*croissant?*
tapping with my stump after hours, a jig at the turnstile
on history's one decrepit toe.

The devil take it. Damned if we're not all, all
stumped by this, what do you call it—this panoply?
this guzzling frieze of innocents.

2

Another bash. Excuse me. It's a carnival, isn't it? Isn't that
what the jubilation's about,
the shoving? Isn't that the curate in his version
of beauty's surplice,
up on that inverted box?

That roisterer with his grin? A paste-up. Marauder or fraud;
I know when I hear an ordinance barked. And that
there's more of him where he comes from,
powderheads, with their heavy boots.

Must we wear these times as a crude emblem, a stigmata?
Like the Day of the Dead, only this is not, surely, Mexico?

Who is that Belgian eccentric, does maskers and bodiless dolls,
infants who look like versions of nobody's ancestors,
a pitiless copy of their owners, poppets in shrunken gowns
who wear a death gaze?

Isn't this just what we've come for, a masque?
A medieval entertainment for our time?

There, that man with a raucous laugh, his cheeks
reddened and puffed from his exertions,
his collar nicked to the jawbone, loose-jowled,
his eyes a saggish cartoon;
that one, Pasty Face, with nostrils battened, neck skewered to a ruffle—
a study in greed and malevolence,
next to the distraught Pierrot.

Makes you wonder, doesn't it, who the mask-maker is, that rogue,
what rustic road he walks, what newspaper he reads,
what precepts he talks,
what taut grin he wears for the glass,
what makes him tick,
how he got his know-how, his credo.

What about his women? Their drapes and their festooned hats?
Why do they seem so imperiled, so grim at their revelry, so rouged?
Besides, their pallor is ghastly.

This town's done up, I give you that. These townsfolk
are up-to-the-minute in witty merriment.
The last town I got to got itself up
in righteous forebearance
like a single cassock, a version of barricade. We barely got out,
what with curfew,
and the continual fusillade.

That's what our time's come to. We've run out of backwaters.

That Belgian? You know who I mean. The chief inhabitant
of his canvas is Death, that grinner, a contrivance.
He's scanning the crush for employment,
like any chiseler about to feather his pocket.

Me? That's me on the left. I'm on holiday with this here, my jilted.
All in the future, of course.

There's nothing to impede us in our revels. You can see that.
Look. We've bought tickets to everything.

3

But everyone is so busy these days. It's hurly burly as usual.
Wherever we queue up there's a mob of us
who get there before even we do,
who are in the vanguard. We are uncertain
when we arrive at the kiosk, just what news to expect,
just what everyone is up to, so sportive.

Rumor has it that a kind of incendiary carnival is on tour,
not just in the provinces,

but right here at the outskirts, our very border.
Small state-of-the art arenas
seem everywhere to have sprung up. But why
are the trailers and broadsides so slow to reach us? We are uncertain
just where the carnival is going to erupt.

Maybe we have lost our gusto for Epic. The street-theatre of our time,
is it possible it's little more than a trumped-up row?

I see it says here, tickets don't come cheap. What history can't scalp
is history's own business. History may need to sweeten the pot.
Haven't we all just about always muscled up the price,
mustered the cost of communal mirth,
whatever the cost, barbaric as it seemed,
ponied up for the antic arts,
chortled from the gallery? Everyone knows who's boffo.
Pistol packers and wiseacres, maniacs and wannabes.

It's a gala all right, with plenty of bubbly,
pickpockets, derelicts, and *name* sleight-of-hand artists.
I suppose that's what a divertissement's for. Still,
the impresarios are at a loss. We have a surfeit
of impresarios. Impresarios
are a glut on the market.
But haven't there always been impresarios,
our rap men, when we look in the mirror?

In another town's town, we hear a carnival is pitching its tent.
The actors are said to malinger,
pale in their extremities, rapt,
while the mob is enjoined by the pitchman
to hitch up for the upcoming inexorable frolic.

Flaubert's Sculpture

                    Peculiarly,
Flaubert
                    was interested
in the spirit of alabaster
as it applies to the most beautiful part of a woman,
her desire,
the feat of its costly alphabet,
its white light housed
in a crenelated tower,
learned in the way sound travels,
spirally,
its white resonance,
its perverse cold cry,

and the various gradual clocks
with their forensic knocking,
in that way, peculiarly Flaubertian, ordered,
with a prodigious memory
for the beautiful.

Blowzy roses in the urn,
perfume of lavishing light
in the cold lamp of the body,
white-nicked from within,
in the niche of the mind's novel house.

The hunger roses swarm, opulent.
And again. I am here. Here.
Here, take your chisel, France,
perniciously to me.

Chekhov's Horse

1

You will have an ensemble for your handwringing,
a devoted family retainer;
the melancholy strum of a zither, the rustle of the summer gown;
things that go off, pistols, lovers;
the reverberation of things that recede:
harness bells, childhood, the voice of the beloved,
things that resonate: the after-breath of an axe, the shaken leaf.

You prefer, don't you, dusk to dust motes, lamplight,
to the gaze of an electric bulb? Samovars. Toboggans.
A goblet that shatters the sensed consequential.
The oblique sentence, bereft of ornament. A woolen blanket
on the swayed back of a carriage horse.

And what is most of all correspondent to wintry days,
a sense of omission.

Because certain characters are intended to be absurd or endearing
does not mean they do not have the capacity
to rattle the bucket with their provincial grief,
their retreating hems,
the shuffle of their handworked slippers,
the collars of their boots,
the scuffed gait at the periphery of the script.

The carriage horse trots on the night path,
a sheath of silver tamped by the Floods.
A Spot replicates afternoon as it blues and subsides,
deranges the moon's course, that melancholy disk
that attends departures.

Tending the flame's stutter does not produce
any very great blaze for humanity. The gown must audibly flare.
The gun must be seen to smoke, the estate to wane
in the ledger, the numerals to totter on the ruled page.

2

Few have remarked on Chekhov's good looks,
his air of unselfconscious intelligence,
his droll mouth, his scrutinizing and humorous eyes
that give you back rueful wisdom of yourself, your battlements,
your comical glint,

but not of the possessor with his dispossessing gaze,
indolent, farcical, disrobing,
his understated sexuality, all the more seductive
for being inexplicit.

What the hands of women do is a reflection of their times.
It is in the effectual flutter,
its authoring, the articulate counterpoint to the face
that their lives speak. Not least,

the lives of the servant girls, little Masha, for instance,
her incessant plucking at her apron,
wringing a flute of its ruffle, Masha. Masha
does not have that inner sense of the flow of rivers,
of the passional change that attends first the effusion,
then the denuding of bodies and trees.

Mme. Récamier's Casket
after Magritte

I would rather sleep reclining so I do not see The Visitor arriving
in his dented bowler, his two-button gloves,
his platinum fob and dilatory chain.

Some lives seem actually to occur in the course of a painting,
or vigil. But the most lively thing in lives
or painting is the sentinel.

Beauty, crooked the way the body is, awaits,
sans breathing holes, sans slats,
poised to put her foot prettily on the footstool,

to drop her wrap, to let her gaze be voluble:
What ravage is to time, I am
to ravish.

Kafka's Vanishing Point

A scaffold where the unfelicitous moon
spills in its nightly clamor
before that imperfect shelter, the body,
imperiled by half-light
as it perambulates the corridor
where soon it is called to remember
the allure of its address,
the house fanning out in the sepulchrous yard,
the apparitions joined in a febrile ruckus,
just as it vanishes, the body,
through a falsifying door,
the latched sound of its homely hinge
gone to rust,
just as the father in his Homburg repeatingly puzzles
his son's whereabouts where
he's theoretically home,
just as a shadow elongates
and slips through the grate, a foreigner
with no meat on its bones.

Dickinson, Bishop, and Stein

When Stein spoke of roses she said it was:

(and Dickinson, of flies
and Bishop, of fish)

Simple.

What do women talk of?
The same thing men do: dying

and being.
It is that simple, the weight of simple

flowers, fish, flies,

the air they displace,
the bright syllables of their breath, their bubbles,

the buzzing around them.

And don't you think gardens in the drowsy season,
and rooms of dust-speckled motes,

and waters seamlessly green are simple enough?

How often does the simple subject
confound our simple grasp?

Ionesco's Gala

When the chairs are set out it's a comedy.

The chairs won't be brought out until the invited arrive,
wearied from the roil.

From a lighthouse, a boat is perceived
with an opposite mind.

What a fray back of the footlights. And the play not even begun.
Hung with our medals, our griefs, our mental rabbit's feet,

we hide our alarm. To be surrounded entirely by water?
Surely, a miscalculation.

We have only to be festive, and to wave our stubs.
La Belle—she is the one with papery skin,

hair piled in a silvery hive, clutch-bag held to her powdery throat.
She is an apparition of loveliness overdue, as lovelies are.

These farces are wearing, I suppose, what with our dolor,
and so many exits. Doors are so flimsy on the stage,

so opaque, don't you think? So ajar? Or, obstructive.
Chairs, too, with their rungs for uneasy purchase.

Doors are thoroughfares for bored actors, ourselves.
A heap of luckless chairs, the bones of what we will have become

when we have vacated them. Half silly
from our witness to imagined rowing,

mosquitoes, and stagnant water, ourselves
implicated, we guffaw. A chortle would be more in keeping.

Backstage, there's a window where the sill drops off
into the parlous lap of water, that addled platform.

Now to get all dressed up
and put on our laughs.

Giacometti's Matchbox

He kept his maquettes from prying eyes.

They had to lie so the wind wouldn't take them,
their long arms bonily private.

They had to prop their feet in order to prevent
any sort of feudal skirmish. They had to be luminous,

as lovers will be, given their chance in what was, after all,
one of the less interesting landscapes—so shady.

They had to try to interest Cézanne, lacking volume and,
lacking color, Gauguin;

to interest Braque in their geometry—they had none,
and Gris, poor Gris,

whose occupation was gray;
and to be inflammable, if possible, in front of Picasso.

They had to elongate themselves to talk, and their voices
were tenuous. They had to whisper, one to a box.

When the box was closed, their solitude
was palpable. They were so gaunt, they were

breakable. You could jab your thumb in the hollows
their maker had thumbed—or your thumb

in the hollows their minds occupied—
sockets for the eyes of their minds.

On their own, they consoled themselves, asking: How is it different
muscular, when the world, small as it is, is contained,

and bones are for scaffold, only, and breath, only to breathe?
They had to be tensile in an interesting way,

and to own up to fragility. And to be luminous,
to light up the dark.

You could have heard them from box to box knocking, asking:
How is it for you to be flammable?

Asking: *Does anyone have a match?*

Mrs. Edward Hopper

crowded Punch right off the docket.

Said: *Flesh of my flesh, bone of my bone,* of him.

Said: *Once I bit him to the bone. I could feel the bone.*
            Eddie's lonesome.

Said: *He married me for my curly hair, my*
            smattering of French, and
            because I'm an orphan.

Said: *I am here, only*
            as a dent in his canvas, an elbow,
            an eccentric presence.

No midnight counter in a small town
where the only window looks out
on the hurt grays of an emptied afternoon,
or room depleted of furniture and
light, or street, scored by the aura of someone
to whom we are arguably attached,
or dune, crisscrossed in our minds
by a zone of no stray,
is uninhabited.

See the curtain blown back at the *deserted* window?
It appears to envelop
a form (as easily,
ourselves, in stilled weather) at the sill of a long-dry canvas or day,
where the shade has been pulled by a cord with a ring,
so no one will know there is nothing, nothing
there absented,
or, to be absented from.

        Flesh of my flesh, bone of my bone

Do not believe this, if you do.

Stravinsky's Biographer

It is so understood isn't it
that there is nothing mathematical
involved

in the calculations required
to reliably
reconstruct the language of strangers

from diagrams and
notations,
however voluminous

and dissonant?

In writing these few memories,
Stravinsky's biographer remarked
that Stravinsky's wife

had said, *No one
speaks Russian anymore.* This had
somehow,

an air of finality.

On occasion, he noted, Vera Stravinsky
would clap her hands, would ask:
Where have they gone? What place is this?

At these times, he would feel, he said,
that he lacked a suitable
tenderness,

an ear for music of this foreign sort.

Sitwell's Friend, Dolores Hidalgo

Dolores Hidalgo, where do you go?
brooding among the epitaphs and symmetric beetles,
elephantine in your constructions,
your meticulously parsed arguments for the reclining,
dead or elevated.

Never mind the concentric circles of parsimony
and averrals—
more graphically, the dust
uninvoked by elders
and interminable dead parsons
with small purses

or bees that multiply
and beat their fevered wings
cacaphonously against the panes.

Are you warming yourself for a divestiture,
as if some mad dog puppeteer
specifically had thrown the leash to reroute cold
that sleeps along your dormant bones
and rouses in your winter mind,

a serene debility,
dolor, Dolores,
a discreet and disjointed disquiet?

Rimbaud's Drunken Boat

I board it, me, sober, with a spyglass.
Nothing's left to debauch.
I'm sickened by the sight of inebriates
And entranced by I can't say what.

My old salt's a tippler.
Some wanton has stiffed him.
They've tangled their mouths.
Like a caustic net.

Under the voyeur moon
That dwindles like a clipped nail,
A meaningless glyph,
Sibilant foam.

I'm afraid of the rapturous creak
Of the boards,
A swift kick from the vast insolid
Under this tilted skiff.

Stendahl's Plot

        Guillotine is a word
that cannot be completely conjugated. One may say,
I am to be guillotined; I shall have been guillotined, but not
I have been guillotined.

        At the heart of these absurd enterprises
we call it our human lot to undertake to suffer,
is an absurdity more central: How to keep in a room apart
a sense of what we know to be,
amazingly,
our fate,
      how,
from the place we think of as home,
we set out ingenuously for the place we're bound,
no head for the contraption,
no ....

O'Keeffe's Bones

                will whiten eventually,
immaculately whittled by a rib from
the wind's cage.

If you come on a bone in its natural state, naturally
paint it. Erotica lives in voluptuous principle: in a marvel interred
in the house of itself,
or abandoned where it immensely resides
in its personal desert,

                or, in ephemera, in detritus claimed
by the elements,
in the obsolescent and in the inflamed,
heroic skull, for example,
lit or lapsed,
exposed and eroded,
that the digger stumbles on and preserves
by shoveling it over, clod by clod,
                or collecting what evidence there is
of the thing having existed at all. Or, reprieves it.
Home, pounds the nail in.

The skull pulsates there. Lights up the wall.
Lights up the canyon behind the hollows where its eyes were.

Is this cause for awe? Haven't we always been keen
to record our passion for the comely dead?

Don't they continually solicit us, solicit us?

Toilers of the Sea

after Ryder

What will has ordered this small boat
tipped into the thrash? No reason,
but thrall.

The gaze of the moon, too harsh to blink,
a defect,
horrible in its fixity.

So much white licks the horizon. The sky is a secondary sea.
There is something alive in it, aboil.
No eel of the stark mind can account for this rampage.

The current is an elbowing Everywhere
with its suggestible magnet. Neither
are the clouds inert.

That is the nether sea. Its impassive face
is the face of the assassin
we toil for, for

what else recurs, and deranges itself
on a painted slick
of roiling foam,

intoxicates every exile
who tilted a sail,
moon-stropped a century ago

in his fervor, a delirious masquer
wearing the mantle
of his indenture

waging to the debited sea.

Sun in an Empty Room

From the stack of books beside my bed,
I thumb some page each night
to help my sleep. I like
to know another juggler's there. Tonight,
it's Hopper. What he painted last, what illusion, what distillation,
what he did to mark each day the sun, that solitaire,
subtracts its deviled patch,
a shrinking rug that leaves no trace,
no horizontal finger.

A footless sound retreats somewhere,
a door is shut,
a shut-in weathers in the room
that hosts the mind, a pallid shiverer.

Something breathes behind the ordinary slat
we call a door. No squabble with a lover,
or world lingers there, or leaks from transoms. But
nothing being heard within's no proof
that nothing's there. Wind slights the real
or imagined glass just the same
as if glass weren't there,
an illusory disjunction between day, and day receding
from the anteroom, or reliquary.

January, that hare, its ruff like a collar spiked
to fend off weather, fate, a talisman,
battery of wind,
its ilk of lies.

Every season has its animal, its animal mind,
its pellucid eye.

What's absented, then, that's worth remark?
An empty room—is that a void,
a negative incapable,
or one, merely, of the vacated events we make myth of,
the bugler tinily taking up
his tiny bugle to his tiny mouth.

The Palace at 4 A.M.

after Giacometti

A rig for the carved tiny spine
suspended in its fanciful cage.

A bird with rictus, or a clown with an improbable nose
has battered itself and hangs from a sketchy bracket.

Appearances are like any other illusion
in the eye of the transfixer.

She makes her perpetual rounds,
bathed by the moon's model mind,

perpetually unconsoled,
obsessed with those women,

their jugulars slit by the sculptor,
in his dream of the oneiric room

for the soul in peregrination,
mourning the original estrangement

any love is.

Rilke's Blue Lamp

Voyeur to their lighted rooms,
satisfied with their lanterns, their silent occupations,
I go among them, expressionless before the glass,
the partition they've invented
to separate themselves from us.

But what are their faces, lit then?
Transparent messengers carting the mind. The smallest
lamp in a single real window
is real. But the imagined lamp has a magnitude
that illumines the distance
between home and home.

I will be obliged to exile myself in order to be exiled,
and to recast the blue light that falls
across what I have kept of myself to myself,
and my shuttered eye with its impeccable memory.
I will have held my hand to the blue shade

and seen my veins like blue culverts
translucent below the surface,
strenuous in their clarity,
and will have inclined my ear to the audible dead, their breath
like stupefied lilies.

I will have dispossessed myself in order to feel dispossessed.
And blue light will have glanced off my cupped palm
with its blue tracing,
and will have spilled ineluctably
across the evening's blue-lined page
even now as I write.

Gertrude Stein's History of Hunger

Someone thinks Paris is naturally gray not really but rather. A nice
color to make up like plaster or puce or lamb too done but nice.
Nice lamb a nice color to eat but not of course have. It is further
you do know gray naturally thinking gray or the degrees of its
absence which it is. To think Paris is to think one dove en croûte
or purée of let us say or say we say lark. What is anything that
anything offers up a winged spirit a gliding feast. Hunger is is it
not a tower of the urgent. This we swear softly. Paris is pretty
well softly is it softly as not. Yes you do like softly you do
like exactly.

All I have said I am going to say. Precision of rhythm. How to live in
the kitchen. History mystery hunger thirst. To get where we must
we must use the ellipsis. The numeral the pleasures of arithmetic
are justly innumerable.

Everything in Paris was thought first to be gray paté naturally escargot
foie gras saucisson statues. Cubes Picasso thought so. Braque
thought so too as much as Picasso. Apollinaire laved gray for his
concrete poems. Sitwell sat down. Satie was sated. And Gris poor
Gris as everyone knows.

Giacometti made gray by erasing it. Left the leavings spindly legs shut
up in a matchbox hardship on holiday. Solitude is an enduring
apprentice. That is the translation. Some would say certainly so
much for the question of how Giacometti did come to make
many bones briefly.

Pastis alas. The grayish pallor of Paris. You have seen too have you in
what passes for winter Giverny by Monet. What is at once
immediately lacking is the nerve to hear what I say. Gray. *Veuve
Clicquot* Monet somehow favored is a ghastly yellow. So is
Cinzano except in Rome where it is for no reason chartreuse.
Profusions of guests. Minus appears magnified in a Japanese
print. Art is a tutor nibbling.

One night all this was not as I have not said in its entirety gray. Before the blue hour ended with Picasso and Man Ray appalled invisibly ink oysters useless for one profitable for two accrued. One by one Duchamp his bride and his bicycle. What hunger is. A journeying to the insatiable. Is time pretty I do not. A good memory is more good than pale ink. Many things happen on paper. Picasso's eye. My mind. Good thoroughly done by Joyce.

One has to go out to go in. Paris is a Morris chair less paisley than floral. Ah voyage. Mauve dusk. Wave close to the glass. A light in the window is where a light should not be. The expired glow. Watch the shapes of to go the rug like a map. Geography with fringe. To the south you will see dust by the fig. Mercurial mignonette. Debate the small life of the olive. I did say such a pass. Art transforms much closer. What bones gnaw the mouth. Sail for Marseille say I. Or didn't I?

Some words do give the idea of themselves. Poussé and plié. A St. Bernard that did not quite give me a fright was called Mousse. I myself saw his arcane collar and his freedom from courage. I have not needed any ruse if it needed me. It is nice to remember pudding and France.

A certain painter painted the scent of a woman. Set the gray scissor. Another the mother and sister. Slit her. Throat slash was good for the history of art. One pummeled them into a matchbox the matchbox into a pocket of the jacket. Paste on the label. The label one by one graduating like certain Russian dolls collapsed on themselves. That pocket was then taken up by the hand of someone whose hunger was to keep it from the eye of Picasso. More to ravish said Picasso.

There is no by the way grass to speak of in Grasse. Very well my
friend Clipsank says Grasse is a business not far from Vence.
Vence is not far from where Vincent viewed his other. Of what
use to Vincent were the two crows that flew up. A teaser the
eye's derangement. At first I did not understand but then I did
completely. Why on the other hand did Freud's patient faint.
I do not care but I do. And so did Giacometti.

You must go with an empty ear famished away. Take your inner
valise. All roads lead to if what happens it. Clipsank says there is
no doorstop smart as a journey. Clipsank says he would rather
think sunlight the length of his arm quake in a foreign bar no
closer to home than have the table laid out inexactly.

I say very well first the old face needs a new wrapper. Think
hometown with its face. Now you see a facsimile now you
see an ellipsis.

Could you need a tassel or a sleight of face. To make a new face the
imposter must be shot. To be seen by the mirror from the back of
your head is to have a front row view of the proceeding. There is
no end naturally and it has never gone out of my hairs to forget it.
Crumbs are a form of raving. Some do see that an idea wants to
be by itself and let it.

Home is where they wait for you to come home. If you live
somewhere else from where are you do. The more you stay
erased the more no more than you should. The mind if you think
it satisfactory is. Spend your mind asking what was that. That
vanished if it did. Home is where the casket is. I myself say
more than I see.

I said I would like to go too with an empty ear away. White paper
whites white napery white light in the alley. Not words but the
sentence of a thing. Pass many bowls of plain violets is not. We
have to say the body is not thing but the cup of our bones old say
so the mind. History's older than that the cheekbones unable
to laugh. Even in France. Art knows its real bones and makes a
pink fresco. Gravity's that. It has not gone out of my mind to
forget it. Thank you for thinking of the ellipsis.

Now utter bones gray with the frieze and the erased thing ragged
on its spiky legs that before you winds down white the wind's
specter crumpled to small scatters as it will the city fled from
within. What flees of necessity hunger and history. No one yet
has feathered this feast exactly. Plaster is a medium of no great
plasticity but opaque it is very. In all towns there is a tower of
the urgent. This we swear softly. It is so the cafe wants to
close its lamp.

III

My Artifacts, My Children, My Parents, My Books

Carnival Days

Show me your red-smeared face drawn gaudy.
The day the war ended, everyone came back mortal.

Tickertape. A blaze of curlicues fell
onto Mother's hat curved like a prow. *Liberty.*

Swains everywhere. I saw
the sailor, hysterical with joy, plant a kiss,

granted, misgauged,
on the side of mother's carnival mouth.

I, meanwhile, clutched the fur of her sleeve,
stared into the hairline, the beadline

of next year, when you, Daddy,
abandoned yourself.

The shades thwanged for years,
those spectrals,

while you crooked your finger at me,
so bony for real.

Plant your kiss here, your seal.
The latent future melds the arrived past.

Welcome, Daddy, to carnival days,
those barkers, those haranguers.

My Artifacts, My Children, My Parents, My Books,
My Continent, My Pond; Hokusai, Paint-Crazy Old Man

1

In this room I say I live in, entire, entirely at home with *my artifacts,* (tucked into frames, as to cribs, photos of children whose names I forget, who left their faces behind, little careless mementos), and with *my parents* raised up from the sepia album, its mouldering breath, a single beard with rime; and with *my books* (the cacophony of their voices makes for a lively jam, nights), in this room, my *inn,* where the neighbors, those characters, clamor, crowding *my desk* with its ledger, the seduction of their blotched names, I am with those I elect. Yet, I wish for solitude, respite. I am under duress from the lives and chatter of *my favorite writers*, and from the reproach of an elongated dent I have preserved on the opposite coast of my bed, that aberrant island, *my continent.*

2

Outdoors, where the dark presides, and is punctual, the ground is a mumble of clots, frost tatted to the berm. The cleft-like hand of a stone holds a tiny pond glazed to its palm. Something in me in the half-lit evenings detaches itself, goes barefoot into the frozen yard like a wraith in a flapping kimono in a *Hiroshige* winter, to stand under the pergola on a mash of leaves, the cup of blues my face is. Out here, where the children in their nightclothes aren't, their nervous laughter natters at the glass. *My mother*, in her peignoir, gracious and stately, pays a visit. We sit on a bench, our feet on a thatch of brittle twigs, while the children caper by the ruined gate, its bolt thrown.

3

Miles ago, Mother, you vacated that other room your house entire
was, left it to me to witness your exit from an ordinary day, the
imperceptible crease the body leaves on a cushion, the newspaper
turned back like covers, the calcified glass, the phone book thumbed
to a deleted name. No one had said air weighs in an unoccupied
space, as in a closet, must intensifies the once animate wardrobe.
A child fingers a knob of the bureau drawer. Fumes of lavender
mumble up. There, amid the underclothing interleaved with tissue,
the candid rose of the sachets, handkerchiefs embroidered with
nosegays, meticulous folds that might be letters of sweethearts died
in the ordinary album, leaves with tattered corners the child rounded,
winters before the wars of attrition—Januaries to come, all
January comes to.

4

Father, lamplight flutters like a trapped moth. January, off La
Cienega. There is no winter in the western south. The stuccoed wall
is a flattered yellow. Fronds of the great palm feather the tile, the
captive moon in the mind's cage. What rap on the Spaniard's iron
grill drew a speechless child to the door? The holly wrap on a book
by the man who abandoned ten children mouldered. We turned out
none of us heroes. But if you stop by this month with four syllables,
tonight we're a good age. Tonight, by the onyx clock, we foregather.
You know everyone, Father. This is Father, weathered from the
dock's wash. Your visage is welcome, Father, however unentire.

5

Hokusai, you knew what to paint *whole,* bone-cold, its tenacity, the
hand of the stone. You were never satisfied. Paint-crazy old man you
called yourself. Here, if you stop by I will show you, let me show you
this smudge on the jamb, the wrought iron knob with its jab of the
maker, you would celebrate that, the throb of a slipper on the ramp,
the implied Japanese bridge, a face and a garden transposed, returned
from the mirror that is a pond, a door, a painting, a death.

Emissary Shadow

It may be that if a father abandons you you will see
 his receding form all your life or his emissary shadow
especially in winter a silhouette with a Meerschaum pipe
 standing under the lamppost with the brim of his hat lofted
in a gesture of affability a wisp of smoke appearing like steam
 under the lamp's light so that the illusory fog that obscures his face
and his stiff collar give you a fright who recognize the revenant
 that lives inside a certain dusk of the season that arrives annually
posits itself on your doorstep with a haggard look its eyes averted
 as if by a scrim so far back the hair must be parted like a wave
so there is no tenant but only a boy on a lantern slide in a homemade
 costume his bugle and plume for the buoyant theatre home
always is where voices reside as a constituency from the time
 when lamps in-gather and the neighborhood starts to subside
thrall by thrall until there are nothing but patches of preoccupied
 yellow on the faces of the houses the windows of their gaze
a blurred glimpse of the fattened sofa the alabaster clock in
 the lit alcove viewed by a florid passerby strolling out of that
dusk toward a certain door above which the number faintly
 numinously shows when dawn burnishes the wall

Dream Enthraller

1

What town does the difference make?
They are alike on the pages of an album
that smells of tobacco and mildew,
imagined dog fur rank from the rain,
and the sepia'd parents that mumble in them.

2

They waltzed in the ballroom with a ratty floor
to music from a tinny gramophone. Beneath the stairs,
in the cranny reserved for children,
he was afraid of the undulate bureau,
the allure of attenuated afternoon.

3

Here's a tricycle wheeled onto the promenade
like a day of its own volition,
a riderless vehicle under a suggestible moon,
sky's infinite freckle,
careening in the calendar.

4

Memory's a murmur the child pedals from,
a peal of body loomed hugely,
emboldened by legend and shadow
and shadow's idolator,
rollicking on the promenade,

a virtual parapet.

Silverfish

I am used to this house that keeps its mouth shut,
this solitary with a liking for the cover of dark—
not half-dark, which is the sadness
of each day's demise,
but dark wholly,
that engulfs the room where mind
cozens up, a guest.

I know this is the hour that nothing sounds
except in the drawer,
and that the articulated physical trill
of the silverfish
as it goes swiftly into the dark
is still not a word.
Its behavior is not a word.

But what is its silverfish breath? Hunger, that rasp.

This disgusts me, but I cannot use the palm of my hand
for its obliteration. Its shadow is too swift.
I am already alone again.

The bystander in the silvered mirror in the hall,
dry-eyed, inured, disturbs me.
I wanted to sever that creature from its life
with a tatter of the day's news.
But already there are too many casual deaths.

I have just learned that mites, those unseeables, do exist.
They thrive on reclusion. They feed on personal detritus
that flakes from the body's case,
a proximate fun-lover,
however frugal or profligate in its thrash.

Mites, silverfish, their visible mateys
that children call bugs,
they make of the game of seek and feed
diabolic employment
to justify mine of snuff or swat.

I avert my eyes and proceed.

Parents

What was I thinking of as I brought children one by one
  into the immense room home was being obliged
to become little by little its roots twined around no trellis but
  the intransigent heart in its attic to repair to to repair
itself when light darkened regularly and the window of each
  oncoming child presented an undecipherable opacity
that grew more dim as we stored up every small truce
  or amend-making and rooted about all of us tenants with no
purchase on the lives we made maps of compasses for dallying
  over the tremorous needle we ourselves caused to poise
at the juncture the uncertain terrain of the palm we
  mutually consulted trying to know something of disparity
unity we could abide each of us lodged in our
  immutable fictions and conundrums too wise to be
clever stunning some truth in us we futilely called desire
  when we meant more subtly longing its permutations
and costs is what so long as I can remember I
  thought in advance of the inexorable necessity of

A Boy's a Double-Jointed Alphabet

1

Every time I see a boy trudging with his dog
alongside some picket fence,
a neighborhood leaps up and impales itself
on the yard of my mind. The one same sun descends again,
a sad map; its veins, local tributaries,
traceless at their source, or a stamp
with nothing to affix to,
its envelope aloft behind the eye,
vocationless.

A student—what is that? One who is not
in possession of his mind,
that gooseneck lamp. A foreign push-pin. A cipher—
something that's a stand-in for what's not there.

2

A boy's a double-jointed alphabet, akimbo for years,
supposed to be a somehow kinetic sort of poem,
lunatic, endearing. Pre-ticketed
for a destination
less exotic than adolescence, more vigilant
than pugilistic.

A boy's an epiphanic grace note on wheels,
a transitory heart-tug, without strings. Not
a puppet politico.

But what's that got to do
with anything? What's he doing
plumped on a moth-bitten chair,
that boy?

3

Not every narrative harbors a dissident,
a country to cower in
without currency. No country wants a fantasist
permanently.

Maybe I'm the mother one
lodged in a fiction, I don't know,
my head knocked silly
to a sidekick's fence,
impaled there.

Let someone pick the hairs off when it's time,
and let it go at that. I hate to see
hairs gray and drift, netless,
so strayed to no purpose,
like silverfish. They make the space they occupy
look somehow unhygienic, ownerless, failed,
while doing nothing virtually at all.

That's their duty. To remind. To flit from no place
to no place,
a hand's length of yards,
unkempt as they are.

But what is distance? So meaningless
to the mother of a man-grown boy.

Other Women

I think of women whose lived-in looks
explain they've gone good distances and back,

gained altitude—whose bodies know
a kind of warrior weather,

women who wear their hair as plumage,
who wing their gaze

from the incandescent caves where they dwell,
women who never sleep,

their nightlife, a stoop, enlivening the district,
luminous in their bones, their shambled digs.

I hold my tenancy as they do,
so traversed, flown,

who know no stoop, no dig beneath
that yawning gap we call a life.

Women, who need to be advised what they own,
their topography, not so different

from that of other women, that expanse,
its little fortresses, orifices,

the space of porcelain and children
allotted to their lives.

Women who do not sleep except in ravaged houses
where night snarls at the latch,

where the dog with a damaged haunch,
there at all, because it had been there

knocks its filthy flank to the mat,
its ear flopped like a flower to a stump,

its gummy eyes in thrall
to the women in wild profusion

whose bones don't speak, who never sleep,
whose children have no encircled crib.

Their thin exhalations leave no stream.
Nothing can be said to be in that house wholly safe.

No mythology. Rain fetters at the glass.
That's the neighborhood other women live in,

imprisoned in their skin. I think there must be
a hut somewhere that lights a window

each dark's descent, as if a vigilant within
held a candle, its flame half-cupped,

and stared out the glass at other women
plummeting past ....

Celebrating My Birthday in Greenwich Village

1

This week, my life took a turn. I'm not ailing. But then,
who knows?

I saw the news, blunt-named, like a strop, blunt-spread,
when I pulled the page from its black mounts.

That is the version of calendar I own,
numbers in their fixed cages, the calendar's zoo.

I saw the days. I saw my linear face, its replications,
the long jaw of my mother.

I saw where it said, *travel* in one of the squares.
So I bought a ticket to one daughter's room

that juts over the ledge of what's left of
the Avenue of the Americas.

I like to think this is where they came
with their one battered valise.

That daughter, years ago, left her childhood, harder passage,
to re-arrive home in a squall, an abrupt immigrant.

Friday becomes indisputably
Saturday. All America careens toward Greenwich,

the village meridian. Pandemonium
is something to believe in.

2

Someone is calling for a Mrs. Coldcut.
I am afraid.

The hearing-impaired neighbors do not hear the barrage,
the intermittent laughs, rant to derange the ear, that amplified tunnel.

I am not deaf to the telegraphed screech
of brakes and vagrants, their pretty mouthful.

Horns blow inanely. Three, four, five joyless riders
rev their broken-down crates

to extinction. The boom-box owners—theirs is a bluff
to thwart the void—joust

on a non-violent plain. Because hullaballoo is Friday's ante.
So are the sirens of mercy and the crackle of glass

my veins leap to,
an uproarious rivulet.

What is that? Howling?
A charitable lot.

I see what my life is going finally toward
after I survive what it's not.

Writers of Landscape, Writers of Place

I've traveled nowhere. I have no town in me
the way they do,
with neighbors alive in the album,
real land to live on in my mind
that winters elsewhere,
vegetation I thumb with pages shut,
no burrows furnished with habitual animals,
no trees whose leaves I know without knowing how,
or nuts by their covert sheath, berries by their tinge,
no season that will shed its skin in front of me,
no natural signpost language,
no storm I read by its vein,
no sky of unstoppable blizzard I remember for years,
no river that bears a private name
by right of my having played on it,
the minute season childhood is,
riven as it is from us,
a scrim,
but only weather anyone can have,
memorized from towns that might as well
have rolled to dust, north and south,
for all they stayed where any house was put,
an only house only children know by heart, one yard, one stair,
one door that opens out, one quarter-hour chime
ensures a kind of sun made sure
in its odd rotation.

I personally knew three beaches, north and south,
junctures as hopeless to possess
as the moment in an hourglass
sand pitches even before it's done.
But I never knew, personally, as western writers do,
anyone, or place, disaster struck, except myself.

Those who have a landscape in their eye
have a place to retire all their lives,
a porch, its yellow gaze switched by a well-loved hand, loved dusks,
when being out was good,
because the way home was safe.
I can't find town, or relatives
who are purported to have lived
anywhere I was,
or Sky, that chart with a face,
a map for how to spend a day, profligate,
sky, that follower on a leash
that thrills every child.

A town child doesn't know for years
what landscape is. By then,
it's buried deep, an Everywhere
that everyone must lose and learn to love again,
a bone gnawed in,
whitened by seasons more of loss
than of celebration.

IV

The Woman with a List

Catalogue and Course Description

Every day but yesterday the lesson is Elemental Attrition
Beginning with the buffeting of raindrops

       Required: No equivalents

For the Fifth day of Fall, credit is offered in Preliminary Mazes

       The elements of mystery examined in three dimensions
       The relevancy of hedging; walls, both anterior and ulterior
       All tunnels, all burrows; the strategy of connections

       No prerequisite: Compulsory

In Winter, all day December, the class is Fundamental Atrophy

       A germinal course on the measurement of windfall
       Study, evaluation and application of control techniques
       Some charting of the dynamics of the bruises of snowflakes

       Progress reports at intervals by certified technician
       Upper level credit to those with sufficient evidence

Next term: Can These Raging Bones Survive?

The Woman with a List

1

      What's she to me, that woman at the crosswalk
skewed to her cane—a linchpin. An imaginary corsage
flopped from her lapel to the curb,
face up, as if endorsed.

There's an archive for you.

      It makes no difference to me
that someone is looking at her
without interest. What's to traverse
in a face?

      And no one loves a passerby—
some simpleton with a carryall,
impervious to winter,
a bland garment a shiver sleeves.

      White Grin, that woman, teeth bared, fronts for others,
so much like an actor, so evasive to a purpose,
as she lists, asymmetric, private in her habitat,
in her original mutter of bones,
among the pedestrians who shamble askew, curb to curb,
that woman among them, glancing in the mirror a shop window is,
oblivious, that woman, so familiar, her list,
an inarticulate remark, a personal jig.

Shall I, shall I? Shall we, shall we?

2

Epictetus, how are you?

Spare. That is a room I rent in my house.
I don't hunger for wallpaper. Let it scatter beauty.
It doesn't interest me the number of petals that must drift to the floor
to denude one rose.
I push up the sash to see what shivers.
As to interior weather, I am indifferent.
Now that it is again evening, I will pull the string that orders the bulb.
I will desire nothing by the usual degree, but to
unlayer myself on my pallet.
Skin that won't murmur. An absence of decor for my mind.
From that hollow the clavicle forms, I will
hardpinch skin,
and pierce with a stickpin what bunches there,
and attach to my naked lapel
the stem of the dropsy rose
for a boutonniere.

A pinpoint of red will prick the white field of this winter house
I call austerity.

A Trap Set by Thieves

A gray woman emerges and hobbles down an alley
  where hollyhocks have dominion their blossoms exposed
for that is expected as everything is that flowers
  that has no possession that sways from stems set on edge
by the passing of noon into an indomitable sea
  for that is the black that envelops it as light emblazons
the body that expectant a nerve in the earth that knots
  itself as the gray woman stumbles at a pace the old child set
for that was the piratical rule where these ideas exist
  in sleepless notebooks reliquaries for the mind susceptible
to thieves and ghosts for that romance is referential bones
  conjugal in their relations no less than certain flowers
but that is hardly proof of love without enfoldment
  of another the bones neatly folded not askew
so the woman proceeds in consequence of the continual
  clumsy forage while ensurers deploy their minions
she is doubtful as she passes through miracles
  the doors of them her smile a sealed envelope sentinel
of its own solitude its enervating existence

Shoring the Scaffold

It can be done of course, if that is what is wanted.
Because, after all, doesn't everything break finally down?
And it is not all that difficult a task to be mistress of an illusion.

The carpentering art, not a Herculean matter, can be mastered,
but what a shambles the body is, its lumbering, its hobble,
its continual comical attrition,

the occasional masque afforded by the collapse
of small unexpendable parts, body's ingenuity,
a design for what will befall it. No wonder

skin is so bracing, keeping the establishment
from exposure, bones from
a concerted lunge. And isn't it useful

to obtain a splint, and other accouterments,
and the technical precision
required to mount them?

But what scaffold is about, is dismantle,
is about something built to be obsolete,
not to self-destruct, but to abandon,

to be carted from the premises,
a primitive contraption. Imagine, in another context,
the taxidermist, his ardor and disdain,

a fiddler with a divinable countenance,
deceptively pliant,
constructing an object to be savaged

in front of an illusory mirror. At the local
junction, a contrapuntal wind
goes hanging about.

Queen of Angels, Providence, and Mercy

I am here on a mechanical matter dozing hooked to the apparatus
  when a rush of waters foreign in its affinity arrives from a great distance
lapping and nipping at my syllables raffish bubbles a commiserative wave
  washes over my attire my bones that other time I debarked discommoded
outraged pinioned splayed swaddled mewling flailing likewise incompre-
  hensible bemused by the receding face a blur with two spotlights that gaze
burned onto a slate where all of this is being continuously recorded the
  interior torrent gate with its grimace its gaping smell the infinitesimal
wheeze inspired graffiti the darling cargo a bleat scurries with
  rustling away the old paraphernalia the stern hem of the minister

The Origins of Assemblage and Bionic Parts

Say it right. It starts with
the breakdown of small parts, unexpendable,
in a foreign town, yourself, a puzzlement, conundrum-like,
a disarray in advance, like the first platoon,
before the final assembly.

It is understood isn't it this simple case
we call the body is a quip,
on the run from clocks with tiny feet,
our heads, bobbing toys?

Well, why say more?
Nature loves to view through a visored slot,
this arcade we call our lives.

Those simple sticks at which-ways
we call limbs, those petty fugitives,
in some, cause bedlam,
archaic as they are, curiously inept,
if replaced—

the hands, worse than crabs for
pincers, petty panhandlers,
the legs, for locomotion,
too bowed for all but deranged games; the knees,
those erotic knobs,

fat where it is not chic to be fat;
the hips, collapsible, as a portmanteau
for traveling small distances
with an interesting lexicon,
as to the floor.

This is called *to dislocate,*
a deviant construct for the body,
not the norm, a ploy for contortionists.
And what is this, a heap, like laundry bunched and forgot?

Let's say the body dropped down
to dodge projectiles, or missives,
cursing and intersecting
like a bumper car

from which a charge emits. It ricochets like a spastic,
a little armored catapult,
clueless at its sport,
like a walker.

And this we call *assemblage*, after the French, who
enjoyed disparate juxtapositions,
disquieted, decades from us moderns
in our streamlined models with

interchangeable parts,
like Tinkertoys, or prostheses,
and other grim gizmos that
are state-of-the-so-called-art.

Art Appreciation, Getting a New Body Part

Days later, in my calendar, or in the book
of Flemish paintings, celebratory,
with my finger's palm, I blot a swarm of crimson daubs
by which Brueghel meant to commend
a host of miscreants at their frivolity,
dwarves really,
propped by a bit of kindling.

Art is the chronicle of history's banquet,
or the feast of Body, its disingenuous passage,
misshapen, at the homely fair,
the rustic village it repairs to at dusk.
But only modern science, a sterile text,
will have me to the window, the eye's marketplace,
to watch from my pinhole camera, the gambol.

See how the pedestrians hunger to be effectual,
small vehicles, their legs go and stop, antic,
their headlamps illumine the heap,
the indistinguishable crumpled forms
of the vanquished. Here's to the tiny survivalists,
to their vivid witness.

Not your average art lover's fault that science, without rancor,
has come up with a devilish glyph
for that faltering piece of work
from which the architect begged off. I hoist my new body part,
white hankie flagged to it, my body surrendered
to the hedonist moderns,
their ardor, their
weaponry.

From Orthopedics to Coronary Care

1

I limp down the hall, a throng.
I will drop in on a neighbor whom I love.
A simple call.

I'm convinced she has no use for us, but she
tries to make her face a model of ours
by watching closely how we do it.

All that was her vivacity has turned against us.
Her eyes wander now. They travel in.
I think I see our faces inverted

on the screen of her eye.
I believe she does not want us here
with our incompetent compassion.

I'm convinced she has no use for us
in the place where she is,
her most vivid remark, a rattled breath.

There is the baleful eye. Her unaccustomed mouth
curls with what looks to be uncustomary displeasure.
I'm afraid she means me. Because I am here.

But it's not possible to know
in what pasture her mind roams,
friended or foul,

trailing thin filaments
that spell into names
she gamely retrieves.

We can't know if she hates us
for being able to be here, when she
is unable not to be.

It's too much for her to call up words.
I will have to call up my own
from a well.

2

I tell her, *There is the pear tree in blossom*
just out the window. Tucked into the bureau mirror,
there you are with your radiant smile
in the snapshot taken last autumn.

Taped to the bedstand is the bride
receding in the frame. We will have to wish her well
indefinitely, time and again.

Someone will try to tell me
how the world poises on the head of a pin
as imperiled as the tiny bride and groom.

Yet the pear tree, just now
so appalled with fruit, its branches bear up,
while the preceding blossoms fail.

I hear my voice thin in the pall. Talk seems inane,
like a round of applause in an emptied theatre.
I am an actor with one toppled line.

I trace my finger on her arm
for her to know I am here. She may yet
have something to say

to whoever has now arrived, who sits fingering her pearls,
another mute visitor lapsed on a chair
preparing her words.

She watches me, I think,
her face a tangle of apparatus.
Her finger, its incongruous red nail

picks absently at the tape
that attaches the tube
to her nose.

I am afraid of her arms like protuberant sticks,
or the branches of the pear,
that carve themselves into the sheets.

This time, time is a century of waits,
sentence without bail. The day goes by
at an atrocious clip

and descends into pallorous dust.
My room is just, is
just down the hall.

Mammogram

Women are not the only ones
who come here to the department. Men, too,
compose themselves around the impassive faces they wear
to ward off the sound of their own two names
called out in front of the ears of strangers.

Here we are, hands compressed in our laps,
or between our legs: Be advised.
It's courteous not to flail. Hands have, after all,
nothing to do but to lapse, or to clasp the magazine,
the magazine cocked.

And, here in the department, there is no lapse
in protocol. Waiting for the film to begin,
the women and men are poised to be vertical,
or, respectfully, horizontal.

What positions we're in, faced with our lives,
our visible injuries less interesting. What *will* be
interesting, will appear to be an illegible smudge
to the novitiate, ourselves.

In regular *film noir*, the gun, that tiresome device, the gat,
will typically be revealed. But, with the high grade
of materials they use in the department,
and such machinery at their disposal,
and such time elapsed before
the concealed is apparent,
there is plenty of time for the smoke to blow rings
around the stunning bruise we sustained
when we were cast for our parts.

V

Ruminations on Concave Water

The Equilibrist's Toys

Put your mind back to never mind which season your year
 forgetfully altered when the streamers spent their luminous
rhythms and the amazed eccentric worm twirled beneath the lamp-
 post made a bow and corkscrew vanished and the little crumbs
the leavings were inconsequent to you were brushed irately the
 equilibrist in you perilous and experimental went to lengths the
high stories and your loquacious pulse and the vibrant rib winded
 you you thumbed daily the volume of antique maxims visited the
vitrine of amulets and statues miniature versions of yourself travesties
 toys on the altar of your anterior life small ceremonies for jocular
weather the insensate complement of injunctions and fetishes
 battering sun bones it warms futilely that can't talk that crying
become the rain balancing along the crucial the set furrows

It Is Understood, Isn't It

that the dead cannot be perfect for it would demoralize the living if
they were if all those blemishes that make what is so human in us
reassuringly human were removed from the register at death
all pocks all scars so that their ravishment would not be so
entirely evident we living left to grapple with ineptitude
and disaster and pitiful mark-making and raucous
laughter more from relief than from acuity
might decline with more gusto for the
terminal magnet of perfectability
who would not be willing to
rush along viscous light
into ether so rarefied
and transmuting?

Dressing Up as Thucydides

I put on a beard. I respect the ancients.

I will be brief.
The fun of conflagration.

A need for kindling is discovered.

What to do for tinder?
Ashes will be a kind of relief.

The wind came up with its heavy broom.
The broom was swift.

The hearth was swept.
History was helped.

Historians staged a simple bonfire,
Simplicity itself.

They fanned it orange.
That's all they did.

Its burnt odor carried to the border.
They have yet to assess the damage.

It was the start of winter.
We women went without heat.

Ruminations on Concave Water

The house consumes its occupant,
An absented woman who does the rounds,
Hungry in her career, muttering to the walls,
Ignoring the jape of furniture
Those overbearing armatures
That clutter her mind,
Its allowable part, a minuscule clock,
And the unenviable calendar
With its forensic bleat
That detains her.

Absence is one bead inseparable on the abacus.
Or a bead of ink in that woman's diary,
Punctiliously asexual
To spare her remembrance
Of the necessary body in its common horizontal,
Its common refrain
From common decorum.
I forget her, the equilibrist on the wire
She traverses absently,
Her mind bisected with its ravishing fevers.

In the rash of summer and remembrance
That disquiets her mask,
She summons the quintet in its murmur, the winds,
That play as one malingering shadow
That jimmies the window to seduce her,
Bookish, irregular in her syntax, an invention of solitude
Like the unaccompanied cellist that persists
Also in pursuit of seasons
And the dissonant chord that is her present voice
Harbored on the page.

Memory's a carouser
That slips through the blinds like a slattern,
A derisive voyeur at the transom,
A voluptuary that trances her, an enamourer, a whisper
That ruins her, self-seeking wanderer
In the circuitry of her house,
That curious repository for relics and herself,
Herself, an invert reader of newsless papers
Whose avidity is a ruse.

Absented woman, mordant, inaccessible,
As a stone is that drops through a crease of water
To survive in another climate,
Crafty sojourner,
To elusive music with no tumult,
Stone like a fist,
Like a terminal clock
Rusting in an armature
Of hungry waters.

The Aperture in the House

Tell them this who talk among themselves
on the enveloping sofas
in the low-ceilinged rooms of the benefited,

that I talk with them, presume with them,
their lives, who go home to the scattering light
of another body and read by it,

and wake to its imprint,
all mercy of audible bones in their jostle,
the audible mind, skin,

a text for hunger, virtually unabatable,
instantaneous and momentary.
Heart, an auditor. Uncredentialed.

After memory of the bestial tumble,
after the turning out of spectrals
in their harrowing remark,

their ancestral mumble,
in the presence of a vaunted sentence,
and the voices of rain, stuttering,

apparitions bereft of ornament, fanfare,
in their bared address I lie, expectant,
as the aperture in the house opens its eye.

Trowel, Spade

for the plot you denied me,

all but tutelage you would extend to a mere flower,
saying for me to watch it unfold,
its transmutation, a flower's transmutation
being something you would like, you said,
to be observant to.

That you found arousing I don't doubt,
its throes, its erratic pulse,
the known course of petals. Their abandon.
Their altered tinge. The stem in its bared state.
The irreversible gasp.

In the climate of a hothouse,
it's difficult to locate a real brief,
to preserve the bloom,
however gorgeous the spectacle
of its original profusion.

And to this, you were averse: memory's preserve.
That bloom's decline, for example,
the drooped amaryllis,
a capsulated version of the process
of tumesce and subside.

Such an exemplary erotic, too. Not like
the dull simplicity of the daisy,
a hackneyed specimen, in all candor.
Likewise, the yokel petunia, because of
its lack of euphony.

Not that it took either of us that short a time to die,
only not prospering, as some do for years,
assuming faces of correspondent docility,
or that the tutelage was not costly—it was,
or that nothing ensued—it did.

But in the hothouse where everything that breathes,
forced to its bloom when the season for its kind is come,
whose conduct is most strict, and in accordance,
regenerates, that is cause to rejoice
and cause to be sad,
because they too are beauteous
in their gradual erosion.

The Mind, Its Dated Statuary

The somber galleries with their niches,
the pale urns, heaped with ashes.
The grave perfume of the beautiful, their transient lives.

The obduracy of things is known.

Stones like a mordant calendar.
The poetry of their grooves.
The sentinel with lids incised,

His moveless pupils implied.

Encampment

The dog bays. That tarp the sky is, with its local moon,
I've traversed, a sentimental watch,
pretending to commune,

because there's nothing else to do with the dark
but walk it, neighbor myself.
The dog has reasons of its own to live.

The arcade on the pier's shut down again
the way it is for children with something they desire,
a small furred thing, a plastic amulet

denied them. I tell myself everything gives itself away,
and clangors down the chute.
Who am I to stipulate?

My hand cups the spout, its hinged flap.
The carnival in me starts up.
A toy rattles in its sphere.

In the crease of my palm
a minute barque
breaks on the horizon.

Notes

Page 3. "The Resonance of Objects Litany": the first line was suggested to me by the poem "Hiéroglyphe" by Charles Cros (1842-1888).

Page 29. "Mme. Récamier's Casket" refers to Magritte's painting "Portrait of Madame Récamier," a remark on transience and the impermanence of beauty; in turn, an allusion to the nineteenth-century portrait of Madame Récamier by Jacques Louis David.

Page 36. In "Mrs. Edward Hopper," some of the quotations are invented; others appear in an essay and interviews with Edward Hopper by Brian O'Doherty that appeared in *American Masters: The Voice and the Myth in Modern Art* (New York: Dutton, 1982).

Page 37. For the idea of Vera Stravinsky's "quote" in "Stravinsky's Biographer," I am indebted to Robert Craft for anecdotal material that appeared in articles, interviews, and two of his books, *Stravinsky: Chronicle of a Friendship* (New York: Knopf, 1972) and *Stravinsky: Glimpses of a Life* (New York: St. Martin's Press, 1992).

Acknowledgments

Grateful acknowledgment is made to the following publications, in which some of these poems first appeared.

The New Republic:
"Encampment"

Poetry Northwest:
"Catalogue and Course Description," "Game," "Punctuation"

The Mind, Its Dated Statuary

The somber galleries with their niches,
the pale urns, heaped with ashes.
The grave perfume of the beautiful, their transient lives.

The obduracy of things is known.

Stones like a mordant calendar.
The poetry of their grooves.
The sentinel with lids incised,

His moveless pupils implied.

Encampment

The dog bays. That tarp the sky is, with its local moon,
I've traversed, a sentimental watch,
pretending to commune,

because there's nothing else to do with the dark
but walk it, neighbor myself.
The dog has reasons of its own to live.

The arcade on the pier's shut down again
the way it is for children with something they desire,
a small furred thing, a plastic amulet

denied them. I tell myself everything gives itself away,
and clangors down the chute.
Who am I to stipulate?

My hand cups the spout, its hinged flap.
The carnival in me starts up.
A toy rattles in its sphere.

In the crease of my palm
a minute barque
breaks on the horizon.

Notes

Page 3. "The Resonance of Objects Litany": the first line was suggested to me by the poem "Hiéroglyphe" by Charles Cros (1842-1888).

Page 29. "Mme. Récamier's Casket" refers to Magritte's painting "Portrait of Madame Récamier," a remark on transience and the impermanence of beauty; in turn, an allusion to the nineteenth-century portrait of Madame Récamier by Jacques Louis David.

Page 36. In "Mrs. Edward Hopper," some of the quotations are invented; others appear in an essay and interviews with Edward Hopper by Brian O'Doherty that appeared in *American Masters: The Voice and the Myth in Modern Art* (New York: Dutton, 1982).

Page 37. For the idea of Vera Stravinsky's "quote" in "Stravinsky's Biographer," I am indebted to Robert Craft for anecdotal material that appeared in articles, interviews, and two of his books, *Stravinsky: Chronicle of a Friendship* (New York: Knopf, 1972) and *Stravinsky: Glimpses of a Life* (New York: St. Martin's Press, 1992).

Acknowledgments

Grateful acknowledgment is made to the following publications, in which some of these poems first appeared.

The New Republic:
      "Encampment"

Poetry Northwest:
      "Catalogue and Course Description," "Game,"
      "Punctuation"